Printed in the United States of America

Image credits:
Hidi's Palace Sukur.jpg - DipoTayo
Don Miguel de Castro, Emissary of
Congo - Jaspar Beckx

Dedicated to
Annu Patti & Siva Thatha
who have travelled througout the
world, and have told some really
good stories about it too!

Table of Countries

Countries - pg. 4-23
Canada: pg. 4-5
Peru: pg. 6-7
Germany: pg. 8-9
Nigeria: pg. 10-11
Democratic Republic of the Congo: pg. 12-13
Egypt: pg. 14-15
Iran: pg. 16-17
Pakistan: pg. 18-19
Japan: pg. 20-21
Philippines: pg. 22-23

Geogractivities - pg. 24-30
Identify the Countries: pg. 24-25
Fill in the Crossword: pg. 26-27
Guess the Country from the Picture: pg. 28-29
Answers: pg. 30

Acknowledgements: pg. 31

Canada

2

Canadian Arctic Archipelago

Beaufort Sea

Alaska (U.S.)

Great Bear Lake

1

Mackenzie Range

Whitehorse

Great Slave Lake

Mackenzie

Canadian

Coast Mts.

Rocky Mts.

Pacific Ocean

Edmonton

Saskatchewan

Lake Winnipeg

Great Plains

Winnipeg

Calgary

Vancouver

United States of America

Fast Facts -
Population: 38 million, or 7 Norways
Area: 6,402,186 sq. mi., or 242
Switzerlands
Ethnic Groups: Caucasian (70%),
South Asian (7%), First Nation (5%),
East Asian (5%), Black (4%)
Language: English, French, Others.

1

Lake Louise is a pristine lake in Banff National Park, which happens to have lots of skiing and glacier tours, and on the way, you might just see a grizzly bear!

4

Churchill, Manitoba, is the southernmost and one of the best places to see polar bears! But be careful – as they have a stronger bite than a great white shark!

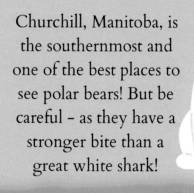

2

3

Alert is the northernmost permanently settled village in the world, and is only 508 miles away from the North Pole!

Ellesmere Island

Alert

Baffin Bay

The Vikings were actually the first Europeans to reach Canada around 1000 A.D. Led by Leif the Lucky, they landed on Newfoundland, but decided to not settle, and returned to Greenland.

Baffin Island

Foxe Basin

Hudson Strait

4

Hudson Bay

Shield
Laurentian Plateau

Atlantic Ocean

Lake Superior

Québec

Gulf of St. Lawrence

Montréal

Newfoundland

Ottawa

St. Lawrence

Lake Huron

Toronto

Lake Ontario

Lake Erie

Halifax

5

5

The Bay of Fundy has tides that rise and fall over 48 feet, or the height of a 5 story building!

Food Corner:
Poutine is a tasty dish with french fries with cheese curds and gravy as topping, and is from the Québec region of Canada. "Poutine" actually means mess in French.

Peru

The mighty Amazon River starts in Peru, at the source of the Mantaro River. In addition, you can actually see <u>pink</u> dolphins in the Amazon River!

1

The Nazca Lines are geoglyphs - giant lines in the Nazca Desert, with some lines being 30 miles long! Some of these draw plants and animals. Look closely - can you see the killer whale?

2

Ecuador

Amazon

Marañón

Piura

Chiclay o

Andes

Cordillera Central

Ucayali

Trujillo

Chimbote

Pacific Ocean

Huancayo

Lima

Mantaro

Cordillera Occidental

Fast Facts -
Population: 31 million, or 8 Panamas
Area: 496,222 sq. mi., or 59 Israels
Ethnic Groups: Amerindian (45%), Mestizo (15%), White (15%), more.
Languages: Spanish, Quechua, Aymara, other Amazonian languages

The Incas who ruled a long empire from Colombia to Chile were from Peru. They didn't have a written system; instead they sent messages using quipus, or knotted strings. Wow!

Machu Picchu is one of the new seven wonders of the world! In addition, is situated on a mountain and has some beyond belief views!

The Uros Islands are home to the Uru people. Built out of the totora plant, these islands literally float on Lake Titicaca, which happens to also be the highest lake in the world!

Food Corner:
Ceviche is a Peruvian dish made of raw cubes of fish mixed with lemon juice, which cures the fish. Furthermore, it is often topped with onions, cilantro, and peppers.

7

Germany

Brandenburg Gate is an iconic symbol of Germany, it was built during the Prussian rule of Germany. The Prussians were known for an extremely well organized and modern army, and the famous Frederick the Great was Prussian.

Oktoberfest is a festival in München that is celebrated by drinking lots of beers, like A LOT. People drink over 7.5 MILLION liters of the stuff!

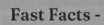

Germany has over a thousand different types of sausages, like bratwurst, knackwurst, and currywurst!

North Sea

The Netherlands

North

Bremen

Dusseldorf

Belgium

Köln

Rhein

Luxembourg

Eifel Uplands

France

Frankfurt

Shwarzwald

Switzerland

Fast Facts -
Population: 84 million, or 14 Denmarks
Area: 221,843 sq. mi., or 6.5 United Arab Emirates
Ethnic Groups: German (86%), Turkish (2%), Polish (1%), Syrian (1%), others
Languages: German (official), others

8

The Köln Cathedral took over 600 years to build. Unfortunately, it was bombed 14 times during World War II. However, it is still standing, and is a beautiful sight to behold.

2

Neuschwanstein Castle is a giant castle and famous icon of Germany. It was the inspiration for the castle that is shown at the beginning of every Disney movie.

3

Denmark
Kiel Bay
Baltic Sea
Rügen
Hamburg
European Plain
Berlin
Oder
Poland
Elbe
Weser
Dresden
Thüringen Forest
Erzgebirge Mts.
Czechia
Böhmer Forest
Regensburg
Donau
Stuttgart
München
Bodensee
Bavarian Alps
Austria

1

3

9

Food Corner:
Schwarzwälder kirschtorte in English speaking countries is known as Black Forest Cake! Filled with layers of chocolate sponge cake, in between are layers of lots of frosting and cherries. Delicious!

Nigeria

Osun Osogbo is a sacred grove dedicated to the goddess of fertility for the Yoruba, known as Osun. There is a shrine in the grove known as Busanyin Shrine, and many drink the waters in front of the shrine, which it is believed to have spiritual properties.

Nigeria has a <u>ton</u> of butterflies. More than 1000 species fly around the country, and new species are still being discovered!

1

Fast Facts -
Population: 231 million, or 5 Spains
Area: 356,667 sq. mi., or 9 Switzerlands
Ethnic Groups: Hausa and Fulani (29%), Yoruba (21%), Igbo (18%), Ijaw (10%), Kanuri (4%), many more
Language: English, Hausa, Yoruba, Igbo, lots more.

Sokoto

Sokoto Plains

Kainji Reservoir

Kaduna

Benin

1

Ogbomosho

Niger

Lagos

Ibadan

Benin City

Slave Coast

Niger Delta

Gulf of Guinea

2 The Gidan Rumfa, also known as the Emir's Palace, was built in the 1400s, and still remains in function even now. The Emir of Kano, Amino Adu Bayero II, still lives here and has a lot of influence.

Niger

Chad

Kano

Borno Plains
Maiduguri

Kaduna

Jos Plateau

Abuja

Benue

Adamawa Plateau

Cameroon

Port Harcourt

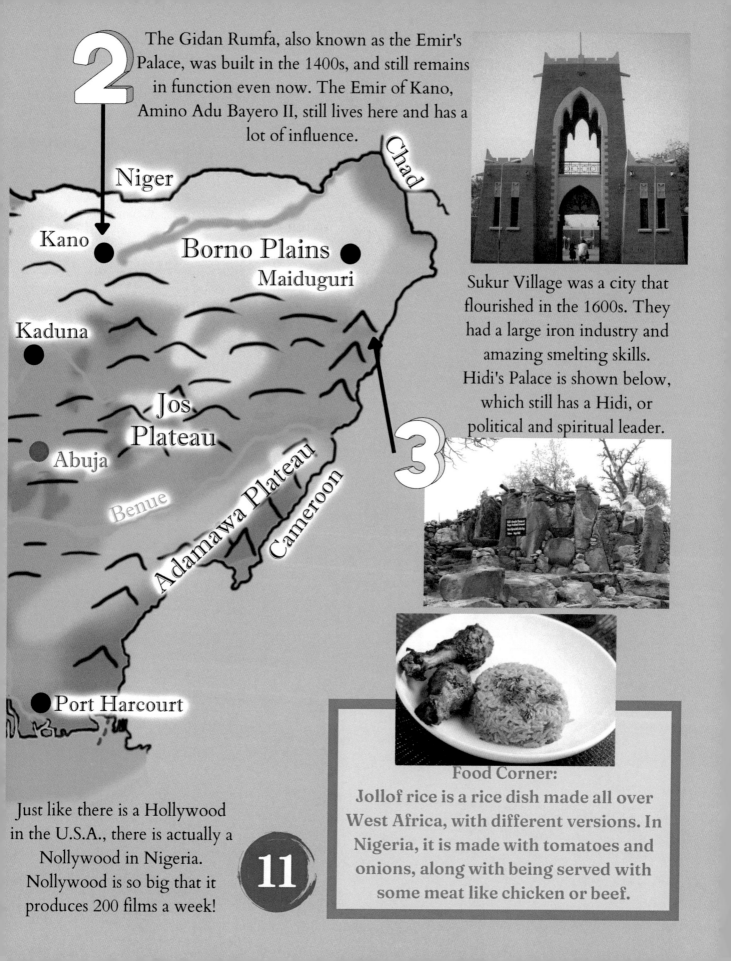

Sukur Village was a city that flourished in the 1600s. They had a large iron industry and amazing smelting skills. Hidi's Palace is shown below, which still has a Hidi, or political and spiritual leader.

3

Food Corner:
Jollof rice is a rice dish made all over West Africa, with different versions. In Nigeria, it is made with tomatoes and onions, along with being served with some meat like chicken or beef.

Just like there is a Hollywood in the U.S.A., there is actually a Nollywood in Nigeria. Nollywood is so big that it produces 200 films a week!

Democratic Republic of the Congo (D.R.C.)

Central African Republic

1

Oubangi

Republic of the Congo

Congo

Mbandaka

Kisangani

Congo

Tshuapa

Lake Mai-Ndombe

Basin

Lomami

Kinshasa

Kasai

Kananga

Atlantic Ocean

Boma

Mbuji-Mayi

3

Angola

Katanga

Kolwezi

12

1 The Congo River is one of the deepest rivers in the world, sometimes reaching 700 feet deep!

Mount Nyiragongo near Lake Kivu has erupted 34 times in the past 140 years. But there's more - there is a giant and deep lava lake in the crater of the volcano. Wow!

2

The Kongo Kingdom lasted for over 500 years and was an influential kingdom. They were in contact with European kingdoms since the late 1400s!

South Sudan

Isiro

3

Rwenzori Mts.

Uganda

Lake Albert

Lake Kivu

Rwanda

Bukavu

Burundi

Mitumba Mts.

Tanzania

Lake Tanganyika

The Lola Ya Bonobo sanctuary is a place where orphaned bonobos are taken care of. Sadly, many bonobos are being killed for meat. Nevertheless, this sanctuary is helping to save them.

This is an okapi. It may look like a half zebra half horse, but it is actually more closely related to a giraffe!

Plateau

Lubumbashi

Zambia

13

Food Corner:
Poulet à la Moambé is a dish that has chicken cooked in moambé; or palm butter along with spinach. The dish is then served on rice or mixed with a cassava paste. Tasty!

Egypt

The White Desert National Parks is quite an interesting place, as over time rocks of chalk have been eroded to make interesting formations. This one looks like a face!

Ancient Egyptians loved board games. Pharaohs and commoners all played games like Senet, shown above.

2

Qattara Depression

Libya

The Pyramids of Giza are the last remaining ancient wonders of the world, and for good reason! They were made of 2 million super heavy stone blocks! Plus, the Sphinx was actually brightly colored when it was made.

Libyan

Sahara

Fast Facts -
Population: 108 million, or 10 Swedens
Area: 386,659 sq. mi., or 23 Denmarks
Ethnic Groups: Egyptians/Bedouin/Berbers (99%)
Language: Arabic (official), French, English

Mediterranean Sea

3

El Iskandarîya
(Alexandria)

Bûr Sa'îd

Israel

Nile Delta

Suez Canal

1

El Gîza

El Suweis
(Suez)

El Qâhira
(Cairo)

Jordan

El Faiyûm

Sinai
Penin-
sula

Saudi
Arabia

Gulf of Suez

Gulf of Aqaba

Eastern Nil

Nahr En Nil

Asyût

(Nile)

Desert

Hurghada

Red Sea

El Uqsur
(Luxor)

Desert

Desert

Aswân

Lake
Nasser

Halaib
Triangle

Bir Tawil →

Sudan

St. Catherine's Monastery, located in the mountains of the Sinai Peninsula, has the world's oldest operating library, having been established in the 500s A.D.!

Cleopatra, the famous Egyptian queen, was actually Greek! However, she learnt Ancient Egyptian and became closer to the Egyptian people.

15

Food Corner:
Egypt's national dish is Koshari. This is a rice dish made with spiced rice and lentils and tomatoes, all topped with onion rings!

Iran

Iran actually has it's own solar calendar, along with using the Islamic lunar calendar and the Gregorian calendar. That's a lot of calendars!

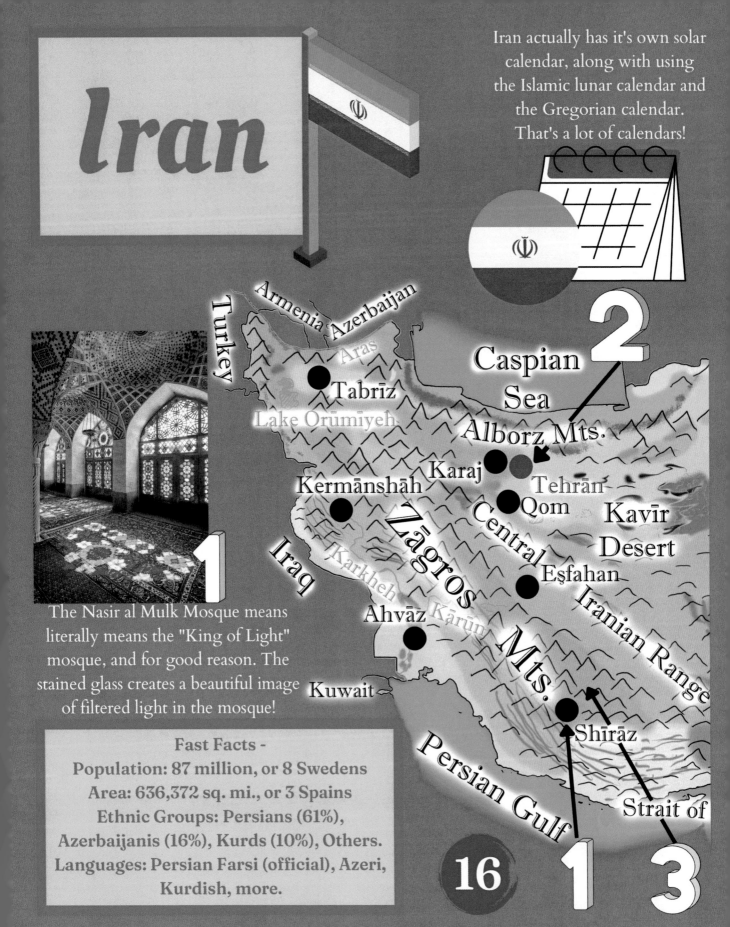

The Nasir al Mulk Mosque means literally means the "King of Light" mosque, and for good reason. The stained glass creates a beautiful image of filtered light in the mosque!

Turkey
Armenia
Azerbaijan
Aras
Caspian Sea
Tabrīz
Lake Orūmīyeh
Alborz Mts.
Karaj
Tehrān
Qom
Kermānshāh
Kavīr Desert
Zāgros
Central
Iraq
Karkheh
Eṣfahān
Iranian Range
Ahvāz
Kārūn
Mts.
Kuwait
Shīrāz
Persian Gulf
Strait of

2
1
3
16

Fast Facts -
Population: 87 million, or 8 Swedens
Area: 636,372 sq. mi., or 3 Spains
Ethnic Groups: Persians (61%), Azerbaijanis (16%), Kurds (10%), Others.
Languages: Persian Farsi (official), Azeri, Kurdish, more.

2

The Azadi Tower is one of the most famous landmarks in Iran. It was built in 1971, which marked the 2500th anniversary of the first Persian empire, the Achaemenid Empire. That is 2 and a half millenia!

Iran actually has it's weekend on Thursday and Friday. That means that in our weekend, people in Iran are working!

ThursdAY frIdAY

Persepolis was built in the 5th century B.C. to be the ceremonial capital of one of the Persian empires, the Achaemenid Empire. Though much was destroyed, there is still a ton of art and writing from that time period.

3

Turkmenistan

Mashhad

Afghanistan

Lūt Desert

East Iranian Range

Zāhedān

Pakistan

Hormuz

Gulf of Oman

Food Corner:
Chelow Kabab is the most known dish of Iran. It consists of chelow, or rice, which often contains saffron; and kabab, or skewered meat, which makes quite a mouthwatering dish.

Pakistan

Mohenjo Daro was a city of 35,000 people that came up around 4600 years ago. The city had an amazing sewer system, multistorey buildings, and a giant city bath!

1

Malala Yousafzai was brought up in an area where girls were not allowed to go to school. She has fiercely advocated for educating girls, and was awarded the Nobel Peace Prize in 2014.

Fast Facts -
Population: 248 million, or 45 Singapores
Area: 494,670 sq. mi., or 14 Portugals
Ethnic Groups: Punjabi (45%), Pashtun (15%), Sindhi (14%), many more.
Languages: English, Urdu (both official), Punjabi, Sindhi, Saraiki, many others.

Afghanistan

1

Quetta

Balochistan Plateau

Iran

Sulaiman Range

Indus Valley

Indus

Hyderabad

Karachi

Arabian Sea

18

3

China

Karakoram Mts.

Himalayas

Peshawar

Islamabad

Rawalpindi

Jhelum

Gujranwala

Lahore

Faisalabad

Chenab

Ravi

Punjab Plain

Multan

Sutlej

Thar Desert

India

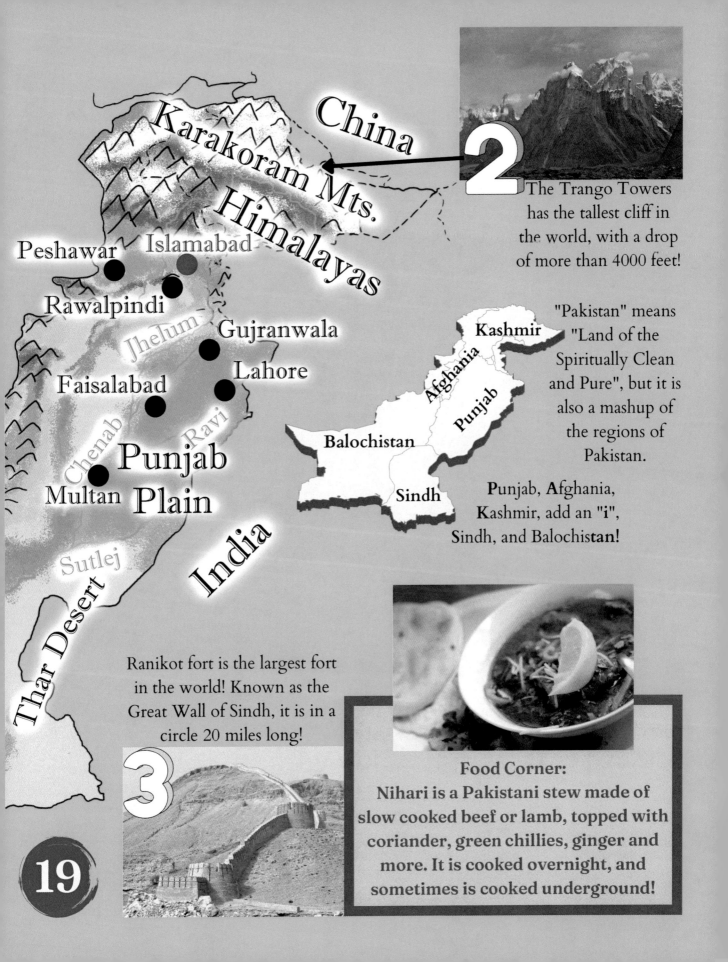

2 The Trango Towers has the tallest cliff in the world, with a drop of more than 4000 feet!

Kashmir

Afghania

Punjab

Balochistan

Sindh

"Pakistan" means "Land of the Spiritually Clean and Pure", but it is also a mashup of the regions of Pakistan.

Punjab, **Afghan**ia, **K**ashmir, add an "**i**", **S**indh, and Balochis**tan**!

Ranikot fort is the largest fort in the world! Known as the Great Wall of Sindh, it is in a circle 20 miles long!

3

Food Corner:
Nihari is a Pakistani stew made of slow cooked beef or lamb, topped with coriander, green chillies, ginger and more. It is cooked overnight, and sometimes is cooked underground!

19

Japan

Mt. Fuji is the tallest mountain in Japan. It is visible from Tokyo, the capital of Japan. Furthermore, it has been an active volcano – it erupted in 1707 and covered the area in 10 feet of ash!

2

Japan has 1500 earthquakes a year! That's around 4 every day!

Itsukushima Shrine is a famous landmark of Japan. Built in the 1200s, depending on the tide of the sea, the bottom of the shrine is overflowed by the sea!

1

Fast Facts -
Population: 124 million, or around 21 Denmarks
Area: 234,825 sq. mi., or 2 Italys
Ethnic Groups: Japanese (98%), others
Language: Japanese

South Korea

Korea Strait

Sea of Japan

Kyoto

Chugoku Mts.

Osaka

Hiroshima

Matsuyama

Fukuoka

Shikoku Mts.

Kyushu Mts.

Kyushu

Shikoku

Russia

Hokkaido

Kidami Mts.

Russia

Ishikari

Sapporo

Japan has one of the highest life expectancies (on average how long one lives), of around 84 years, compared to the world average of 73!

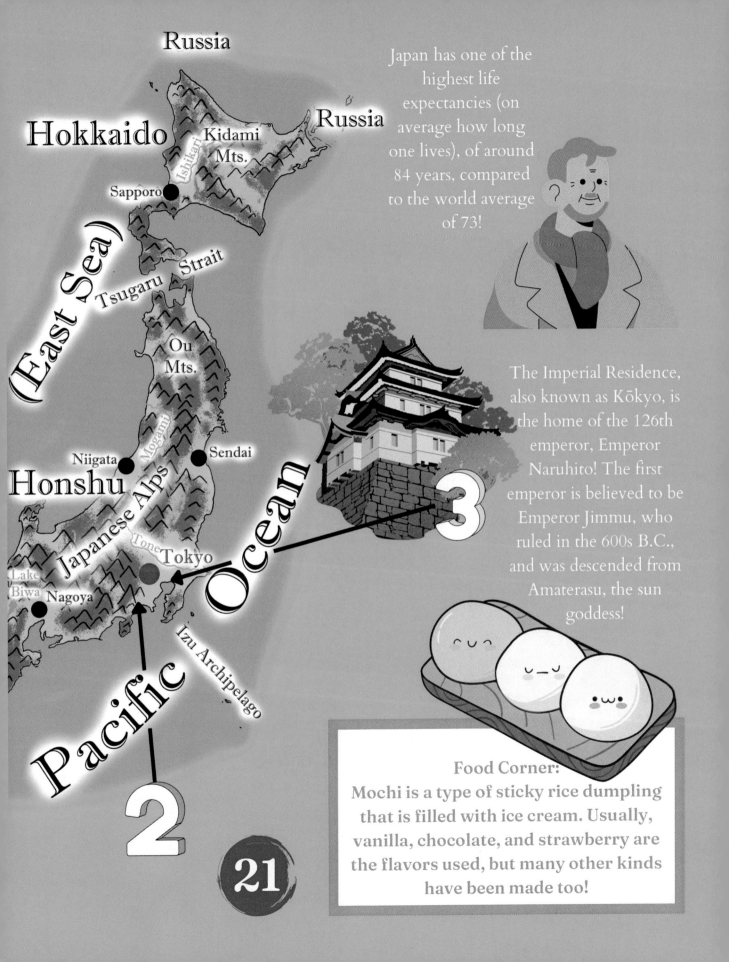

(East Sea)

Tsugaru Strait

Ou Mts.

Mogami

Niigata

Sendai

Honshu

Japanese Alps

Tone

Lake Biwa

Nagoya

Tokyo

Izu Archipelago

Pacific Ocean

The Imperial Residence, also known as Kōkyo, is the home of the 126th emperor, Emperor Naruhito! The first emperor is believed to be Emperor Jimmu, who ruled in the 600s B.C., and was descended from Amaterasu, the sun goddess!

3

2

21

Food Corner:
Mochi is a type of sticky rice dumpling that is filled with ice cream. Usually, vanilla, chocolate, and strawberry are the flavors used, but many other kinds have been made too!

Philippines

The Puerto Princesa Underground River is one of the new seven natural wonders of the world, and for good reason. It is the longest travelable underground river in the world!

The Philippine eagle, also known as the monkey eating eagle, is the national bird of the Philippines, and it is true – it can eat monkeys.

1

Cagayan

Luzon

Cordillera Central

Baguio

Quezon City

South China Sea

Manila

Laguna de Bay

Mindoro

Palawan

Puerto Princesa

Sulu Sea

Malaysia

Fast Facts -
Population: 116 million, or 3 South Koreas
Area: 186,411 sq. mi., or 6 Irelands
Ethnic Groups: Tagalog (24%), Bisaya (11%), Cebuano (10%), many others.
Language: Filipino (based on Tagalog and official), English (official), eight major dialects

Mt. Mayon is an active volcano that erupted just in 2019. The story goes that there once were 2 lovers, Magayon and Panganoron. However, they were tragically killed. When they were buried, the grave turned into Mt. Mayon, with Magayon representing the mountains, and Panganoron the clouds.

The Chocolate Hills are a set of more than 1000 perfectly conical hills, named for the grass that turned brown on the hillsides. Legend has it that 2 giants threw boulders and sand at each other – and the hills are what is left of it!

Camiguin Island has more volcanoes than towns! To be specific, there are 7 volcanoes, but only 5 towns!

2

3

4

Pacific Ocean

Sibuyan Sea

Samar

Panay

Iloilo

Cebu

Tacloban Leyte

Cebu

Negros

Bohol Sea

Cagayan de Oro

Pulangi

Mindanao

Davao

Zamboanga

Celebes Sea

Indonesia

Food Corner:
Adobo, named after the word adobar which in Spanish means marinade, is a dish of chicken marinated with vinegar, garlic, black peppercorn, soy sauce, and bay leaves. Delicious!

Some Geogractivities

1. This country has their weekend on Thursday and Friday.

_____

2. The name of this country can also be an acronym for the regions in the country!

_____

3. The okapi, a zebra-horse like creature related to a giraffe, can be found here!

_____

4. This country was home to the Inca Empire.

_____

5. The Puerto Princesa Underground River, the longest underground river, is here!

_____

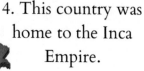

24

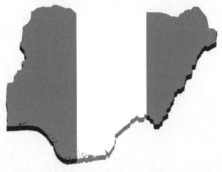

6. This country has a giant movie industry, producing more than 200 movies a week!

_____

7. This country has over 1,000 types of sausages!

_____

8. This country has the northernmost settlement in the world!

_____

9. This country has one of the highest life expectancies in the world!

_____

10. Cleopatra was the queen of this country.

_____

Fill in the
Crossword:

Hints:

Across:

1 This country has an island with more volcanoes than towns!

2 This country uses 3 different calendars.

3 There is a place here where you can see pink dolphins!

4 This country has around 4 earthquakes a day!

5 This place has a giant lava lake!

6 This place has more than 1000 species of butterflies!

Down:

1 This country has the tallest cliff in the world, at over 4000 feet tall!

2 This place has the northernmost town in the world!

3 This place is home to pyramids made out of 2 million super heavy blocks of stone!

4 This country has a beer festival in which 7.5 million liters of beer are drunk every year!

Guess the Country from the Image (Challenge):

1._____

2._____

3._____

4._____

5._____

6._____

7._____

8._____

9._____

10._____

Answers:

Identify the Countries by Their Flag:

1. Iran
2. Pakistan
3. Democratic Republic of the Congo (D.R.C.)
4. Peru
5. Philippines
6. Nigeria
7. Germay
8. Canada
9. Japan
10. Egypt

Guess the Country from the Image:

1. Egypt
2. Iran
3. Canada
4. Nigeria
5. Germany
6. Philippines
7. Peru
8. D.R.C.
9. Pakistan
10. Japan

Fill in the Crossword:

Across –

1. Philippines
2. Iran
3. Peru
4. Japan
5. D.R.C.
6. Nigeria

Down –

1. Pakistan
2. Canada
3. Egypt
4. Germany

30

Acknowledgements:

I thought my journey through OCD was over after I had finished the first book and OCD therapy. But it was like breaking through ice - while it was incredibly intense, there was still a lot of cold water to go through, which for me was going back to school and social life. First I'd like to thank my friends who helped me come back into school - Neal, Nishanth, Karina, Lexie, and Allison - you guys mean so much to me. I want to also say an extraordinary thanks to Chenxi, who introduced me to Blender, a software that has been an amazing help in my mapmaking. But most importantly, my parents need to be recognized. They have supported me all the way, and there is no sufficient way to thank you, mom and dad, for that. But I hope my book has gotten close.

Made in the USA
Middletown, DE
16 October 2023

40443545R00018